Crush! 2008

100 south african wines to drink now

GW00632179

Michael Olivier

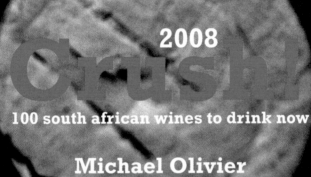

2008

Crush!

100 south african wines to drink now

Michael Olivier

Photography by Russel Wasserfall

For Madeleine, my partner in life and in wine,
and co-producer of our two great vintages
Amy 1981 and Peter 1988.

Published by Gwynne Conlyn Publishing
in association with Jacana Media
10 Orange Street
Sunnyside
Auckland Park 2092
South Africa
+2711 628 3200
+27 84 222 1002
www.gwynneconlyn.com
www.jacana.co.za

Copyright author Michael Olivier
Photography Russel Wasserfall
Design Petaldesign

ISBN 978-0-9802786-0-6

CONTENTS

FOREWORD
NEIL PENDOCK, RESPECTED WINE COMMENTATOR

Like the Springbok rugby team, the great South African wine drinking public is not short on advice. Wine competitions are packed with foreign palates that trumpet themselves as "the most authoritative" because they include no SA buds. Others, loaded with beer-drinking winemakers, give you the technical view from people who would never dream of buying the bottle in question.

Some annual guides charge producers an entry fee and claim to give consumers unbiased advice while others press-gang. Once a year chairmen of wine producers, highly paid industry consultants, PR luvvies, waiters, retailers and lonely hearts all rate bottles, labels in full view, handing down the vinous scriptures, Moses-like from Mount Anorak.

In between all the hype and bathos and PR waffle of SA winespeak, simple facts evaporate. Price, availability and the honest beauty of the fermented fruit of the vine disappear in a blizzard of capsicum, cassia and esoteric debates about acceptable levels of Brettanomyces contamination and the joys of linearity. While just about everyone has something to say, the opinion from the kitchen is conspicuously absent from the annual wine recommendation circus. Common sense would agree that what chef thinks is very germane as the palate that constructs a dish can surely inform on what to drink with it. Michael Olivier spent his first lifetime as one of the country's most respected chefs and his honest descriptions and personal reflections, scattered like tiekies in a Christmas pud, make Crush a user-friendly guide in the maze of SA wine.

If the cost of the bottle is important, if a food match is welcome, if you drink the stuff rather than swirling, sniffing and sipping, and you are allergic to pomposity and posturing, read on.

THE INTRODUCTION
AND HOW IT ALL WORKS

"What should I be drinking? What's the newest wine? What's your favourite wine?"

The typical scenario is a wine shop stocked to the daunting rafters with bottles with alluring labels. *Crush* will tell you, the wine lover what to drink in order to get great enjoyment out of wine without the smoke and mirrors.

The mystique and elitism of wine is all puffery. You don't need a degree in some esoteric subject to enjoy wine.

Wine is simply to be enjoyed. If you like sweet red with fish, go right ahead and drink it.

So – *Crush* is about you, the wine drinker. It's not about stars, medals, cups, accolades – it's about getting the cork out or screwing the top off (that's another whole debate on its own) and enjoying what's in your glass.

This is the annual 'top 100' that tells you what's out there and what you should be drinking at every occasion; whether you're strapped for cash, looking for a middle of the week wonder, out to impress (the boss or your in-laws) or splashing out for an occasion. (Imagine if it's only the two of you on a beach or on a hill watching the sun go down.)

I do hand out some awards, since competitions often miss out on some great stuff – and I don't want you to miss out on them. So look to The Crush Awards for some guidance.

The section on The Raw Material offers some notes on the main varieties grown in South Africa. I feel there is enough info to make you talk sensibly about your favourite grape and who is making a lovely little wine from it. Buy the wines and become familiar with what the grape can offer.

No one producer is favoured over another here; it's your enjoyment that I have taken into consideration.

Each year I taste hundreds of wines – these all said "Wow!" to me – some a loud orchestral and choral Wagnerian WOW and others a single violin Air on a G String wow – I hope they do for you, too.

So get the cork out, screw off the top and get quaffing.

Note: The vintages given for each wine are those being sold at the time of going to press. Recommended retail prices rounded off to the closest Rand are given by the producers at source. Prices in wine departments in Pick 'n Pay and other supermarkets, and specialist wine shops may differ.

Michael

Please visit my website www.noshnews.co.za
or email me on info@noshnews.co.za

THE CRUSH AWARDS 2008

Celebrate with me the wines and the people who make exciting tiles in the mosaic of wine and food

THE WINE OF THE YEAR

Landskroon Paul de Villiers Reserve 2004

Being well known as a producer of Port, Paul de Villiers of Landskroon, where he is the fifth generation winemaker, has access to Touriga Naçional, which he has used to great effect in this wine which – gets my nod for the Wine of the Year. Half of the blend is Shiraz and the remainder is made up of Merlot, the Touriga and a splash of Cabernet Sauvignon.

Elevated in the cellar with great care, the fruit was regularly pushed below the surface of the fermenting wine to extract as much of the essence of these grapes as possible giving it a full flavour profile. Malolactic fermentation took place on oak staves; the harsher malic (apple) acids break down into softer lactic (milk) acids. Oak staves add the elegant wood and vanilla flavours. Its full body is made up of warm and generous sappy fruit and aromatic spices. The American oak used in combination with the French barrels is perfectly integrated into the wine and gives it a 'sweet' edge which is enchanting.

A lovely glass which will find a perfect partner in a richly flavoured casserole, roasted or barbecued beef, lamb or venison - hey and even a burger. I could happily drink it on its own after dinner by a log fire.

What is even more enchanting is the price as it comes in at under R50 a pop.

The 2005 vintage of this wine was released in July 2007.

THE WINERY OF THE YEAR

Flagstone Winery is owned and operated by Bruce Jack.
The puckish, enchanting, amusing, erudite, articulate
and indefatigable Bruce Jack along with a formidable team of
talented people.

Flagstone has been called the most exciting winery in South
Africa. What it does is to produce a range of stunning wines at
almost every price point possible, from the entry level Cellar
Hand Chenin Blanc to the über premium Mary le Bow.

None of these wines appear among the one hundred in this book
simply because they are all so worthy of being included in each
section and I could not have 40-plus Flagstone Wines
dominating the book.

Bruce Jack runs his winery by the seat of his pants, and from
the front seat of his car. He answers emails at 2am (that's in the

morning). He writes copy for his own website and newsletters, for the back labels of his wine bottles, in the most shining use of the English language honed at St Andrews University in Scotland and resulting in a Masters degree in English Literature. He makes his wines with the consummate skills taught him at the Roseworthy Campus of Adelaide University in Australia.

Wines which are divinely food-friendly have a wonderful mouthfeel and are utterly deeply delicious. Flagstone's vineyards stretch from above the frost line, almost on the snowline in the Swartberg and right down south almost to the southernmost tip of the Continent. He will buy all the Pinot Blanc grown in the Helderberg and make the oh-so-easy to drink The Field Day. Or just the grapes grown on stubby windblown vines by Francis Pratt in Elim for The Berrio Cabernet Sauvignon and The Berrio Sauvignon Blanc. Or the mixed specially planted vineyard of three grape varieties owned by Angela Frater up in a Kloof in the Robertson Valley from which he makes the Mary le Bow. Or in Spain where he and his Winemaker Wilhelm Coetzee make three wines in three different areas.

That Bruce is supported by his very special Penny and his parents, David and Elspeth, is evident in the energy he and his team put into the Flagstone wines.

If you've not done yourself the favour of drinking a Flagstone Wine, I urge you to do it now. Go on, put the book down. Go out and buy one or two.

De Wetshof Bateleur

THE WHITE

Danie and Lesca de Wet of De Wetshof Estate in Robertson are masters at Chardonnay. The De Wetshof Bateleur is a blend of barrels specially selected by Danie in his cellar. It is the characterization of everything that is totally wonderful in a superbly fruited, brilliantly wooded Chardonnay. The French oak he uses for just a sufficient length of time to support the wondrous fruit – and the fruit is not overtly citrus as one would expect. There are ripe white fleshed peaches and toasted macadamia nuts all wrapped in the creamiest silkiest of vanilla spiced mantles and an almost marine kelp type minerality. This wine has no corners and no edges, it is quite simply magical.

THE RED

Meerlust Rubicon 2001

This has to give it a head start: drinking a wine in the kitchen of Meerlust with a vine-stump fire glowing on the large hearth, in the comfortable company of the current incumbent, devastatingly charming Hannes Myburgh. For dinner, Betty Brown's chicken curry, steamed basmati rice and sweet cinnamon pumpkin mash, large home baked loaves and slices from a large slab of dark brandied, generously-fruited cake.

Rubicon was the first classical Bordeaux blend launched in South Africa in the 1980s by Nico Myburgh, Hannes's father and his then winemaker, Giorgio dalla Cia.

2001 was the one year in which new vines were coming into production and the percentages of Cabernet Franc and Merlot were lifted – the Cabernet Sauvignon dropped producing a classic minerally wine with powerful savoury not sweet fruit. The tannins are present in fine and elegant form adding to the flavour complexity of the wine.

To have the current winemaker, the youthful Chris Williams, talk me through it, added so much to the enjoyment of my red wine of the year.

THE BUBBLES

Simonsig Brut Rosé

I was with Johan Malan on Simonsig one day when he had just done the disgorgement of the wine that would become Simonsig Brut Rosé.

I got my nose close to the top of the glass and felt my nostrils being tickled by the fine bubbles rushing to the surface. I was bowled over by the fruity smells of strawberry and cherry. I have drunk this wine with sushi, with smoked salmon, with strawberry shortbread and crisp white fleshed peach pastries and it goes down as easily with one as it does the other.

Beautifully packaged – as beautiful as any French Champagne house and as good or better than many I have tasted. This is a wine for festivity and fun.

THE SWEETIE

Monis Vintage Muscadel 2000

Monis is one house which knows not only how to make great sherry (another underrated wine in this country), but this year launched, for the first time in about 15 years a wood matured, vintaged Muscadel. This wine lay gently maturing in 500-litre, old French oak barrels in the Monis cellar in Paarl watched over by master winemaker Dirkie Christowitz.

A full, sweet, unique wine made from red muscadel grapes from the Breede River Valley. Amber ruby in colour with smells of muscat, sun-dried Orange River sultanas, Christmas cake spices and orange stollen flavours. I just love the soft silky rich mouthfeel supported by the oak woodiness, and the flavour that lingers.

CHEF OF THE YEAR

My chef of the year is Peter Goffe-Wood of PGW Eat. Pete is the most consistently wonderful cook – his food is so honest, so fully flavoured, and gutsy, and always pushes the boundaries to create greater excitement. I have had my knees under a table carrying Pete's food in a number of venues on several occasions in the last year and each has been a major sensory experience.

He surely makes the creamiest of risottos, cooks ostrich and venison and beef to utter perfection; his cheese reaches optimal ripeness as it touches your plate – as does any fruit he uses. His ability to match a dish to a wine is unsurpassed except by his ability to match a wine to a food product.

Pete and his wife Elize run a catering and food consulting company and cookery school, (Kitchen Cowboys) in Salt River – or Salt Riviera as they will have it. A course for the ladies is offered, called Girls on Top. Nothing is too much trouble; they will cook anything, anywhere, and at times at the shortest notice.

That they are both special people and great characters adds muchly to the interest.

THE RAW MATERIAL

These are the major varieties used in South African wines, and a couple of the more interesting minor ones too.

THE WHITES

SAUVIGNON BLANC
Pronounced: "Sew-veen-your-Blonk"

South Africa's most popular white grape variety by far when consumed as a varietal wine, though ranked fourth in terms of white grape varieties planted in South Africa. Used for mainly dry white wines, some of them wooded in oak barrels, with great examples coming from Duncan Savage of Cape Point Vineyards, Bruce Jack's The Berrio from Flagstone Winery and Neil Ellis of the eponymous Neil Ellis Wines. Generally they are at their best when young, fresh, crisp and dry. Though there are some outstanding examples of aged Sauvignon Blanc from Klein Constantia and other top marque vineyards. Very successful as carbonated bubbles from the House of JC le Roux.
It looks: bright white with edges of straw and lime green tinges when young.
It smells: aromatic and famously put in New Zealand like "cat's pee on a

gooseberry bush", nettles, herbaceous, hot flinty stones. Warm tropical fruit in warmer areas.

It tastes: crisp, green and lively, herbs, green peppers, green figs. Made in two styles, one stony steely flinty, herby. The other, rich Cape gooseberries and tropical fruits.

It's great with: quite versatile it goes particularly well with pasta and even with fairly tart, tomato-based sauces; fish, shellfish, spicy Chinese or Thai food, asparagus and salads.

CHARDONNAY
Pronounced: "Shar-don-nay"

Arguably the greatest white wine grape, Chardonnay has its home in Burgundy, France where it is traditionally fermented and or matured in oak barrels. It has its detractors in the ABC (anything but Chardonnay) club, but in my opinion this is not justified any longer. Our more serious winemakers have older vines producing grapes with greater character – and they have learnt to be gentle with their usage of oak. There are some superb un-oaked Chardonnays like Danie de Wet's Sur Lie, Peter Finlayson's Sans Barrique and the Juno Chardonnay. Oaked yummies for me, are Danie de Wet's De Wetshof Bateleur, David Finlayson's Glen Carlou, Peter Finlayson's

Bouchard Finlayson Missionvale Chardonnay, Adi Badenhorst's
Rustenberg 5 Soldiers. And there are more! They reach venerable age – über
premium wooded Chardonnays can easily spend six years in the bottle, with
some of the French classics lasting for 30 years or more.

It looks: full straw colour – ranging from a gentle yellow hue, lemon-yellow
white, and mellowing with age to a golden yellow.

It smells: straw may show on a lighter Chardonnay; forest pine or resin can
be part of a simple Chardonnay. Melon, white fleshed peach, citrus, buttery
brioche and vanilla.

It tastes: melons, peach and apricot aromas (which lead you astray and hint
at Chenin Blanc) are often found in unwooded Chardonnay, as are the green
herbs you associate with Sauvignon Blanc. A good unwooded Chardonnay
reveals its citrus fruit – grapefruit skin oil, lemon and sometimes lime,
retaining these characters while young. The wooded ones reflect the
influence of barrels by way of vanilla, butterscotch and toast.

It's great with: wooded ones – buttery dishes, Hollandaise sauce, fish and
chicken dishes in creamy sauces, shellfish, ratatouille, salads dressed with
nut oil. Medium-bodies complement crayfish, smoked salmon or salmon
trout, sushi or Thai food, mild curries, rabbit, chicken or turkey. The lighter
ones, as for Sauvignon Blanc.

CHENIN BLANC
Pronounced: "Shenin-Blonk"

Unfortunately known until fairly recently as the workhorse of the wine industry. Simply because it is resistant to disease, is so versatile and is used for the production of anything from the driest of 'lite' whites like the big selling low alcohol Drostdy Hof Extra Light, through semis and full sweets, bubblies to Lyn Mossop's brilliant Axe Hill Dry White Port and the almost iconic Nederburg Edelkeur, Gunther Brozel's botrytised Chenin which gave rise to all the Noble Late Harvests you see on the shelves today. Some serious players are the multi crowned Forrester Meinert Chenin – FMC – by Ken Forrester and Martin Meinert, anything by Teddy Hall from Rudera, Bruwer Raats and great value Chenins from Bruce Jack at Flagstone with his Cellar Hand Chenin, also Jeff Grier of Villiera and Paul de Villiers of Landskroon who produces a dry as well as an off dry.

It looks: clear and delicately coloured when young, moving to straw yellow and gold when older or sweeter.

It smells: like ripe guavas or tropical fruit, melons and delicate honey and flowers.

It tastes: white fleshed peach, apricots, guavas, melon and honey.

It's great with: seafood and Thai food – or light summer chicken dishes.

RIESLING
Pronounced: Rees-ling

Described by Jancis Robinson, compiler of the Oxford Companion to Wine as *"the greatest white wine grape – poor old Riesling, the most under-appreciated and mispronounced grape in the world".*

Riesling is the wine grape of Germany, and makes some of the fruitiest and most sublime wines. Known here as Weisser or Rhine Riesling because we can't put just Riesling on the label. Some serious examples coming from Bruce Jack of Flagstone with his Frostline Riesling, Paul Cluver, Klein Constantia and De Wetshof.

Riesling is actually the incorrect moniker for Cape Riesling, a French grape – Crouchen Blanc. Theuniskraal and Nederburg Paarl Riesling are best known, crisp, fresh, dry and ephemeral.

SEMILLON
Pronounced: Semm-ee-yon

The second white grape of Bordeaux and becoming more evident here. Charles Back of Fairview, Marc Kent of Boekenhoutskloof and Andre Rossouw of Constantia Uitsig regularly produce crackers, as does Bruce Jack with his four star Jack and Knox Green on Green Semillon. Arniston

Bay has one blended with Sauvignon Blanc which is yummy. Lots of flavour, low in acid, oily, charred toast and minerals.

GEWÜRZTRAMINER
Pronounced: Gher-verts-tra-meener

Rose petals, litchi, frangipane all scream Gewurz which is German for spicy. Usually made sweet like the Simonsig Noble Late Harvest which has a nose like a perfumer's workshop, an unctuous full sweet & sour apricots and pineapple. Though the drys – Paul Cluver and the Altydgedacht – are both lovely food wines.

VIOGNIER
Pronounced: Vee-yon-yay

Southern French in origin and often blended with Shiraz for added aromatics. Vernon Cole of Ridgeback offers a stunner (and a blend with Shiraz called His Masters Choice). Bellingham The Maverick has fat peaches apricots and spice and the Fleur du Cap unfiltered is well oaked with soft sundried cling peaches showing through.

VERDELHO
Pronounced: Vurr-day-lee-oh

Found a delicious one in Johan Malan's cellar at Simonsig. The wine screamed fish and sushi. The same grape used by the Portuguese for Madeira and White Port, also their *vinho verde* wines. It can be found on the shelves of Pick 'n Pay only, as one of their exclusive wines. Bottled in a clear glass bottle (known as flint in the trade) with a screw cap to retain its freshness.

MUSCAT – Alexandria, Morio Muscat and Muscat de Petit Grains
Pronounced: well, Mus-kat!

Floral hanepoot, great in sweeties and fortifieds like the Landskroon Morio Muscat Jerepigo and the Monis Wooded Muscadel. Some of the most underrated wines we make in the Cape, and they're usually given away. Klein Constantia Vin de Constance is in another league, along with Groot Constantia Grande Constance – both replicas of the wine which made Constantia wine famous in the 18th and early 19th centuries.

THE REDS

CABERNET SAUVIGNON
Pronounced: Cab-bear-nay Sew-vee-nyon

Cabernet Sauvignon is King. Cabernet Sauvignon's home is Bordeaux. In South Africa it is bottled as a varietal on its own, and there are some superb examples – Jeremy Walker's Grangehurst Cabernet Sauvignon Reserve, deep, dark, then rich and succulent. Etienne le Riche's eponymous Cab, so luscious, broad and deep, Danie Truter's concentrated Onderkloof Cabernet Sauvignon and Mark Lindhorst's wonderful blackcurrant fruited, cedary Lindhorst Cabernet Sauvignon. It is blended with Merlot as in Flagstone's Bowwood and sometimes with Pinotage and Shiraz.

It looks: dark red ink, you're hardly able to see the light through it. Purple round the edges while young, brick as it ages

It smells: blackcurrant, plums, dark Tayberries, pencil shavings, cigar box. Like your grandmothers oak linen cupboard.

It tastes: Like heaven. Full-bodied, incredible breadth of flavour, blackcurrants, dusty tea-leaf, chocolate and even mint.

It's great with: roast beef, casseroles, grills – marinated or heavily sauced – as well as stews, kidneys, venison.

SHIRAZ
Pronounced: Shirr-azz

Legend has it that Shiraz, originated in the town of the same name in ancient Persia and landed up in the South of France where it achieves greatness in the wines of Chateauneuf du Pape. Not a prolific bearer, it is South Africa's third most popular variety for drinking.

There are some local gems: Bruce Jack's Flagstone The Dark Hourse, Stellenzicht, Zandvliet Estate's Kalkveld Shiraz, Boekenhoutskloof and Fairview among them.

It looks: dense ruby extending to the rim in recent vintages. Brick-coloured russet edges may start to show with age.

It smells: fruit, fruit, fruit. Smoky, pepper and spice fragrances and wild herbs. Older styles can prompt thoughts of savoury venison, fine Italian leather and tar.

It tastes: Shiraz typically has red berry fruit intensity, plum, a spicy pepperiness and a sweetness on the palate which is reined-in with top examples. Rustic farmyard flavours can be noted. Fudge and candy-floss can be found, especially if winemaker blends back or ferments with a touch of Viognier.

It's great with: red meat dishes with sweet and spicy overtones; venison, oxtail, ostrich, bredies and goulash.

PINOTAGE
Pronounced: "Pea – no – taarzjh"

Beware the person who says he doesn't like Pinotage – he's immediately accused of not being a patriot. I was talking to a well known Australian wine maker and international judge and asked him what he thought of Pinotage. His response? "I don't believe it will ever be anything other than a curiosity outside of South Africa, rather like Californian Zinfandel."

Of South African origin, this Pinot Noir and Cinsaut (Hermitage) cross (by pollination not by grafting as is commonly believed) was engineered by Stellenbosch University's Prof Abraham Perold in 1925. Years later some vines were discovered in his garden. The first commercial bottling was a Lanzerac 1959 released in 1961.

Pinotage was really made famous in South Africa by Jan Boland Coetzee and Beyers Truter at Kanonkop in an all-singing, all-dancing whopper of a wine. Fat with fruit and oak. Bruce Jack's Flagstone Writer's Block flies the flag brilliantly, whole berries crushed, lovely tannins. Beyerskloof with its sweet American oak sappiness is a favourite of mine as is Schalk Burger's Welbedacht Pinotage Barrique Select which has a wonderful minerally fruitiness, beautifully backed by oak. David Sonnenberg's Diemersfontein Pinotage – the people's Pinotage, as he calls it, is all Starbucks with its now well known, coffee and chocolate on the nose, and palate.

It looks: deep ruby to plum in the centre. Carmine to brick red and purple at the edge. Almost orange brick around the edge when older.

It smells: red berry fruits like mulberry, strawberry and at times raspberry and bramble. Spice box adds to the many layered nose. Nail varnish whiffs are less common now, as is the distinctive banana and pawpaw peculiar to certain Pinotages. Smoked meat and salami can also be picked up and the newer styles show good quality French and American oak.

It tastes: a young Pinotage will be packed with ripe fruit and spicy plum flavours and a jammy character if very ripe. Medium to full bodied usually, and often finishing sweetish. Some styles can tend to the Pinot Noir side of the cross like the Bilton Pinotage. Spicy raspberry, cherry and strawberry fruit carry through from the nose, as can hints of tropical banana.

It's great with: unwooded, fruity Pinotage goes well with game, lamb, bobotie, braaied boerewors, fish, curry and young cheddar. The more full bodied wooded ones match well spare ribs, pepper steak, or full flavoured game dishes such as ostrich, kudu, springbok and guinea fowl.

MERLOT
Pronounced: Mare-low. In the USA they say Murr-low.

A classic grape from Bordeaux – usually blended with Cabernet but does well as a single variety here in the Cape.

This is the slice of Christmas pudding, the plum cake which 'fattens' out the more austere elegance of Cabernet. Usually lower in tannin and acid, it is food friendly and also a great glass without food. Some of the excellent Cape examples are Bruce Jack's Fish Hoek – huge chunks of berry, soft and food friendly, John Loubser's Steenberg, John Grieve's Avondale and Chris Keet's Cordoba.

It looks: much like Cabernet Sauvignon.

It smells: like blood plums and the sweet spices of Christmas pudding.

It tastes: soft, elegant, plummy, food friendly wine.

It's great with: duck, guinea fowl, ostrich and good sausage. Merlot can also be good with curry – especially if the curry is a more traditional sweet Cape Malay curry rather than a hot Thai or Indian curry.

CABERNET FRANC
Pronounced: Cab-bear-nay Frarnk

Used in Bordeaux as a blending wine in the great Bordeaux blends.
A parent of Cabernet Sauvignon (the other is Sauvignon Blanc). Lovely
deep red and black fruit with mushroomy turned forest sod aromas. Look for
Norma Ratcliffe's Warwick Estate, David van Niekerk's High Constantia and
Bartho Eksteen's Hermanuspietersfontein Swartskaap. Bruwer Raats makes
a really delicious one.

PINOT NOIR
Pronounced: Pea-no-nwahr

The red grape responsible for some the greatest wines of Burgundy.
Used in Champagne production with Chardonnay. There are a couple of
gems to be found in the Cape – Bruce Jack's Flagstone Fiona, Achim von
Arnim's Haute Cabriere, Danie de Wet's Nature in Concert and David
Finlayson's Glen Carlou. The Paul Cluver, Elgin Vintners and the two
Bouchard Finlaysons, the Buitenverwachting and Klein Constantia show
that a cooler climate can be a distinct advantage.

Lesser known reds. Watch out for these to add to your taste experiences.

Mourvedre – Spicy, meaty and successful in a blend. In Spain, Flagstone's Bruce Jack uses it in a delicious blend he calls La Bascula Turret Fields. Good locals are Beaumont, Spice Route and Fairview.

Malbec – From the south-west of France and transplanted to Argentina where it is a star. Local yummies come from High Constantia, Signal Hill and Bellevue.

Sangiovese – Used in Chianti Classico and well used here as single varietals in Piet Dreyer's Raka, Fairview and L'Omarins's Terra del Capo. In a blend the fabulously drinkable Boschetto from Stellekaya and Bouchard Finlayson's wondrous Hannibal.

Barbera – Another Italian, high acidity and low tannins, great with food. Altydgedacht and Fairview both have top notch offerings.

Tinta Barocca – Portuguese port variety and used here for Port-style wines and also excellent dry reds. Allesverloren and Swartland, both from warm vineyards are good drops.

In *Strapped*, as in strapped for cash, I tell you about 25 wines which over deliver at their price point when you run out of money before you run out of month. Every day quaffers at more or less every day prices. Some perhaps not exactly entry level, but offering great pleasure and reasonably.

Boschendal Blanc de Noir, 2007, Paarl

I was working at Boschendal in the vintage in which this wine was made and was part of the launch team of what became and remains the Cape's benchmark Blanc de Noir. A white wine, by legal definition, made exclusively from black grapes. Not too serious a wine, onion skin pinky brown in colour, made from a number of red varietals, berry fruits predominate, super lunch time wine with salmon or smoked fish. Good stuff if you have a river and a punt on it, lazily floating. Or lazily lying under a willow.

R35

Brampton Shiraz, 2005, Stellenbosch

Adi Badenhorst has added splashes of Mourvedre, Viognier and Grenache to his Brampton Shiraz making it a real Rhone Ranger. This vintage was in the top ten in the Pick 'n Pay WINE Magazine Shiraz Challenge in July 2007 and comes in tops at a price point of under R50. Fat flavours of ripe bursting berries, brilliant, brilliant oak shining through. Just a sensational drop from Rustenberg, South Africa's 'first growth' wine estate.

R48

" Fat flavours of ripe bursting berries, brilliant, brilliant oak shining through ""

Buitenverwachting
Buiten Blanc, 2006, Constantia

Hermann Kirschbaum makes over 50,000 cases of the Estate's entry level wine a year and many, particularly those up in the Constantia Valley use it as their house wine. Mainly Sauvignon Blanc with a dollop of Chenin Blanc, it is a no nonsense fruit and flowers, *lekker* glass of wine. At the other end of the spectrum, the Buitenverwachting Christine is the 4½ star flagship red and, for me, one of the great Bordeaux style blends of the Cape.

R38

Chateau Libertas, 2004, Stellenbosch

Stellenbosch Farmers Winery in 1925 was founded by an American named Winshaw, whose descendants still live in Stellenbosch. His Chateau Libertas, launched in 1932, has been occupying a loved place on the shelves and on wine lists for over 75 years. The 'Old Faithful' is mainly Cabernet Sauvignon, filled out with Merlot and Shiraz and a splash of Malbec. Food friendly popping berries and softish tannins that'll make your taste buds ask for the next mouthful. William Charles Winshaw's legacy lives on.

R25

> **The wine is a beautiful salmony colour with strawberry and crunchy watermelon flavours**

R35
Delheim Pinotage Rosé, 2007, Stellenbosch

When one thinks Pinotage Rosé, you have to think Delheim. Each year when the new vintage is released, I think, "Ah Delheim time again". The 2007 - screwcapped, Hooray – has a touch less Muscat this year and is a tad drier than before. It's moving into more serious Rosé territory. The wine is a beautiful salmony colour with strawberry and crunchy watermelon flavours – try it with a watermelon and feta salad. Great on its own as a refresher in summer. Fabulous Delheim Grande Reserve and Vera Cruz Estate Shiraz from the Sperling family. *Pater familias*, Spatz was a founder member of The Stellenbosch Wine Route in the 1970s.

R25

Du Toitskloof Sauvignon Blanc, 2007, Worcester

The first 2007 Sauvignon Blanc to hit the shelves. Good stuff and utterly charming. Delicate of body and an easy drinker as it's not totally dry. Flavours of tropical fruits like granadilla and roasted pineapple. Excellent value winery, one thing the cellar does really well is turn out two great sweeties, a Hanepoot Jerepigo and a Red Muscadel, a bottle or two of which can always be found in the pannier bag of my friend wine writer David Biggs's Vespa Scooter on trans Karoo trips to beat off the cold.

Fairview Sauvignon Blanc, 2007, Paarl

R39

Screwing the cap off and releasing the wonderful waves of pink grapefruit oil and rhubarb aromas is a most inviting thing. That the wine is fresh and full and tastes as though the roots have had to go far down to pull up the minerally tastes, takes the appeal further. A great whack of acid will match most summer foods and get the juices flowing. Nice concentration and extract from dry land vineyards. Charles Back does it yet again.

> **"Not unlike some of the wines from the Veneto, fattened up by lying on the lees for a while"**

Flat Roof Manor Pinot Grigio, 2007, Stellenbosch

R35

In Italian grape variety, called by a well known British wine writer 'the new Chardonnay'. This is uncomplicated wine which I find so easy to drink. There is an element of fun with the label too, it's the Flat Roof of Uitkyk, that beautiful Thibault town house on the slopes of the Simonsberg, and there's a cat lurking on each of the labels. Not unlike some of the wines from the Veneto, fattened up by lying on the lees for a while.

R43

Glen Carlou Tortoise Hill Red, 2005, Paarl

David Finlayson produces wines of depth and stature. Pinot Noir, Chardonnay, Syrah and Grande Classique amongst them and his cupboard is full of medals for each one. Tortoise Hill Red is a multi layered and oh-so-drinkable mélange of Cabernet Sauvignon, Zinfandel, Shiraz, Touriga Naçional (a Portuguese Port variety) and Merlot. As you get your nose into the glass there are strawberries dipped in dark chocolate, spiced with cinnamon. Really ripe red berries more raspberry than blackberry and more of the sweet spices swirling round your mouth, round and silky as you swallow.

" **David Finlayson produces wines of depth and stature** "

Mrs Cloete of Groot Constantia was well known over a hundred years ago for her van der Hum, a liqueur she made from naartjie skins. Boela Gerber builds those aromas and the flavours of dusty herbal fynbos into his zippy SBS. One of the Cape's more captivating young winemakers, his Grande Constance is a replica of the famous sweet Muscat Constantia wine drunk by the crowned heads of Europe. He's no slouch when it comes to fine reds either – get a cork out of the bemedalled Groot Constantia Pinotage 2005 and the Groot Constantia Goewerneurs Reserve.

R44

Groot Constantia Semillon Sauvignon Blanc, 2006, Constantia

R55

Ken Forrester Chenin Blanc, 2006, Stellenbosch

Ken Forrester is the prophet not recognised in his
own land. He's known as Mr Chenin here – even
his car number plate says Chenin. Accolades and
awards pour in from over the waters for his wines
– especially the FMC, an über Chenin he makes
with Martin Meinert. This Ken Forrester Chenin
Blanc is both fermented in, and rests for 9 months
in French oak. Spaanspek and white fleshed peaches
undertoned by the well integrated toasty oak with
a hugely delicious, food friendly, zippy ending.

Krone Borealis, 2002, Tulbagh

Nick and Mary Krone weave magic at the top end of the Tulbagh Valley turning out one of the best value for money classic Champagne method bubblies around. Krone Borealis is easy to drink, soft on the palate, the bubbles shout fun and you're in the mood before the delicious wave of Chardonnay and Pinot Noir hits your palate. Chardonnay lending gravitas and the Pinot Noir red berry flavours so enchanting in youth, yet the wine will age with extreme grace if you can bear to keep it. Their lovely strawberried Rosé Brut Cuvée is further proof that they know what they are doing bubblewise.

R60

Mark and Christine Stevens used to provide us with organic vegetables for our restaurant before they took themselves off into the Slanghoek Valley to make superb organic wines and plough their vineyards with Percheron horses, whose deposits help with the fertilization. On a good day – and probably on a bad day if the truth be told – Mountain Oaks is pure magic, you just don't want to leave. This is a real luncheon Chenin under the trees, wondrous aromatic melon, sliced ripe pear, honey, and frangipane with a mineral tip. Best taken with a handful of Christine's organic almonds.

Mountain Oaks Chenin Blanc, 2006, Slanghoek

R35

R49
Mulderbosch Chenin Blanc, 2006, Stellenbosch

Mike Dobrovic would not take it amiss if I call him eccentric. His Friday morning email poetry just brings the week to the end on the right note. His wines from his Chardonnay through red blend The Faithful Hound and Sauvignon Blanc are all top notch drops. This Chenin, which is gently enfolded in oak to enhance the fruit and flowers indicative of the grape, is one of my favourites – a touch of sugar, it's not quite dry, adds to the charm as does Mike's skillful use of American Oak for a vanilla edge.

" **Be a devil you Chardonnay and Sauvignon drinkers, surprise yourselves** "

R35

Nederburg Rhine Riesling, 2006, Paarl

Riesling suffers from not being appreciated. This is a perfect food wine. Sure it has a touch of residual sugar though it's just on the other side of dry; its spice, its acidity, its mouthfeel mark it a real partner to oriental foods, Chinese, Thai, Vietnamese as it does to the full colourful flavours of the Mediterranean. Be a devil you Chardonnay and Sauvignon drinkers, surprise yourselves. Nederburg has the experience with this grape – as it has with many others – to produce the goods. Never a disappointment for me with a Nederburg wine.

R40
Overgaauw Sylvaner, 2006, Stellenbosch

With resolution, dedication and purpose Braam and David van Velden each year turn out the Cape's only bottled Sylvaner. Green melon dusted with spice on the palate, white fleshed peaches sprinkled with fresh grated ginger on the aftertaste. This is a fish wine – fish in a pan with foaming butter, lovely crisp caramelly bits, with a lemonsqueeze and chopped parsley, sea salt and milled black pepper and cool, cool Sylvaner.

Perdeberg Chenin Blanc, 2006, Paarl

Chris and Judy New, friends who've farmed on the slopes of the Perdeberg for years, have provided their best Chenin Blanc to this under-the-radar winery. Perdeberg's Chenin is one of the Cape's best kept secrets and the reserve version won a gold medal on this years Old Mutual Trophy Wine Show. Plenty fruit of the tropical kind on the nose and in the mouth in a dry zippy wine - food friendly, swimming pool on Sunday morning friendly, "*I want a good glass of wine*" friendly. The pricing is brilliant too! Their Perdeberg Smooth Soft Red at under R20 a pop goes down so easy, too.

R22

"don't tell anyone about the price in case they wake up to it"

Interesting grape, Ruby Cab, cross pollinated from two varietals at the Davis Campus of the University of California. Carignan, a southern French grape able to withstand the heat, and Cabernet Sauvignon which gives it class. Producing a wine which has large chunks of red fruit, soft soft soft and oh so easy to drink. It has a charming sort of berried dustiness to it, a bit like mulberries eaten off a tree. Robertson Winery does a superb job with this grape as it does with other reds and indeed whites too – but don't tell anyone about the price in case they wake up to it.

Robertson Winery Ruby Cabernet, 2006, Robertson

R21

R35

Klein Steenberg Sauvignon Blanc, 2007, Constantia

John Loubser's Steenberg entry in the Platter guide is almost completely written in red. He's just so good at making anything from the grandest of reds to the most sublime of whites and such yummy bubbles. But for me it is in this wine that he excels for he is able to produce it in quantity yet maintain the quality and all the fabulous flavours that a cool climate vineyard like Steenberg can produce in a Sauvignon – the crushed green fynbos aromas and crisp watermelon skin dryness with a zippy food-tackling acidity.

"the juicy soft grapes, sweet ephemeral spices and enough flavour to give it a nice long tail"

R39

Stellekaya Boschetto Rosso, 2004, Stellenbosch

Stellekaya's Ntsiki Bayela has done it for me with this wine. Clever blend of mainly Cabernet and Merlot with a swirl of Shiraz and Sangiovese – the latter making its presence felt in this brilliantly fruited quaffer. The 10 months in third fill oak just shining through gently amongst the juicy soft grapes, sweet ephemeral spices and enough flavour to give it a nice long tail. This is pasta with *salsa al pomodoro* wine, *pizza* with tomatoes and anchovy wine and seared tuna wine. Stellekaya, Italian/Xhosa for 'home of the stars', has produced a *campione* here.

R22
Swartland Tinta Barocca, 2006, Malmesbury

Swartland's Tinta Barocca always makes me think of a red wine sauce I used to make for steak – it has the guts to make a good one. And if it is true that the wine you cook with must be one you can drink, this one has oomph in the glass. A Portuguese port variety from a warm climate vineyard provides lots of fruit and grippy tannins. Swartland's recently released 2004 Vintage Port provides punch with a strong cup of coffee and a petit corona after dinner. The Idelia, their flagship red blend is a whopper too, just like a healthy Swartland farmer.

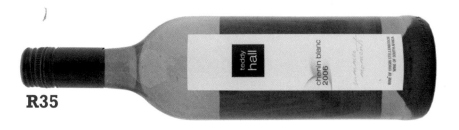

R35

Teddy Hall Chenin Blanc
Summer Moments, 2006, Stellenbosch

Teddy Hall is a winner of the Diners Club Winemaker of the Year Award for
Chenin Blanc, a member of the Cape Winemakers Guild, in fact an über
Chenin maker. His 2006 Summer Moments Chenin Blanc is another triumph
– screwcapped to retain freshness, yet there is gravitas here. Seriously
extracted – a real essence of excellent Chenin from old bush vines. It is so
'meaty' and minerally savoury it will hit a duck breast sideways on and
tackle an ostrich steak happily. Also excels with smoked chicken breast or
hot smoked trout as it is fabulously, tropically, fruity.

> **Seriously extracted – a real essence of
> excellent Chenin from old bush vines**

> **" Such a thirst quencher – and brilliant for those late summer evenings helping the dust to settle "**

Van Loveren Light White, 2007, Robertson

R20

It's become a bit of a tradition that the van Loveren Light White is the first wine of the new vintage to hit the shelves, almost before the presses have been washed out. Lovely, lemony, lanolin wax, Semillon. Such a thirst quencher – and brilliant for those late summer evenings helping the dust to settle. The four Retief Cousins make the well known 1.5 litre Four Cousins Natural Sweet Rosé, one of the top seller supermarket wines. They took a gold medal this year on the Old Mutual Trophy Wine Show for their Reserve Chardonnay 2006. Versatile bunch the Retiefs.

R30

Organic though a good wine first. Some
of the Chardonnay aged in oak to fill out
the palate, which is already inhabited by
white fleshed peaches, honeysuckle and
litchi flavours, with a bit of toasted brioche
with vanilla butter. Excellent Cabernet
Sauvignon and Shiraz too from the
same cellar.

**Waverley Hills Semillon
Chardonnay, 2006**

R30

The Wolf Trap, 2006, Franschhoek

Marc Kent of Boekenhoutskloof's utterly delicious screwcapped red blend is going like a steam train in the UK. No delusions of grandeur, just good honest wine. Flavours tend to be more Rhone than Cape or Bordeaux, sappy chunks of fruit, delicately spiced, sun dried plums wrapped in the toasty vanilla oakiness. It's so smooth and easy to drink, better take two bottles with you to the pizza and pasta shop – you'll finish the first before the pizzas and lasagna arrive.

Middle of the week wonders. **Pay a bit more perhaps for the bottle you take out to your local favourite restaurant or to drink at home with summer salad, a plate of yummy pasta or a winter stew.**

R63

Allesverloren Tinta Barocca, 2006, Riebeeck Kasteel

Drinking this wine at lunch in the Allesverloren Manor House with Danie and Juanita Malan, served with a beautifully roasted duck breast was a special occasion for me in 2007. Danie's favourite grape, from this cool slope of the Riebeeck Kasteelberg, is knockout stuff. There is generous and deeply delicious Port scented fruit, ripe and round with an exciting acidity, giving it a wonderful lift in the long chocolate and spiced coffee ending. Excellent 1997 Allesverloren Vintage Port was released at the lunch if you can get your hands on a bottle for a porty treat.

R53

I am so amused by this wine. Named as a joke, by the late Sydney Back, after the former GM of Backsberg, the crusty, direct and lovable John Martin, who disliked wooded white wines. Screwcapped (hooray) with the almond brioche nose notes of new French Oak it reveals pink grapefruit oil smells and tastes overlaid with Pink Lady apples, ripe green melon and fresh herbs. The limey acidity is in perfect balance with the sliced ripe pears and green fig found in the wine.

Backsberg John Martin Reserve Sauvignon Blanc, 2007, Paarl

R38
Boplaas Touriga Naçional, 2005, Calitzdorp

Carel Nel is making – and then giving it away at the most amazing price – this so different dry red from one of the most sought after Portuguese grape varieties, Touriga Naçional, tiny berries packing punch. Smells deliciously porty and of the almond marzipan my grandmother made. Imagine drinking dry mulberry syrup with just out of the oven almond biscuits. Soft and smooth, and very European in flavour, no wonder Mr Parker gave this one 86/100. Look out for their sensational Family Reserve Sauvignon Blanc, quivering like a greyhound before a race, brittle and zippy, sweaty nettles and a great whack of fruit – the 2007 is serious stuff. Great, truly great, Port from Boplaas too.

> **There is an element of the 'cat's pee on a gooseberry bush' description given to some Sauvignons which I so enjoy**

R55

Clouds Vineyards Sauvignon Blanc, 2006, Stellenbosch

Bernard Immelman is fortunate to have his farm bang next door to Thelema and also to have his single vineyard Sauvignon Blanc made to his specifications by Gyles Webb in the Thelema Cellar. Soft sundried apricots and roasted pineapple accompanied from first taste to last by a bracing lime squirt acidity. There is an element of the 'cat's pee on a gooseberry bush' description given to some Sauvignons which I so enjoy. Great food wine.

Constantia Uitsig Chardonnay Unwooded, 2007, Constantia

R59

Andre Rossouw uses the cooler climates of the Constantia Mountains, marine breezes coming over the top from the cool Atlantic and from False Bay during the summer evenings to great effect with all his whites and his Constantia Red, all made with him by John Loubser in the Steenberg Estate Cellar. Two Constantia experts making delicious Constantia wine. This one has the citrus and butter appeal of Chardonnay with no intrusion from oak, freshness of acidity, full of flavour both in breadth and in length.

R50

For his 2005 Sauvignon Blanc, Giorgio dalla Cia was the first South African winemaker to replace cork with the Guala Seal Elite, a hi-tech, man-made composite closure that has all the properties of natural cork but without the risk of cork taint. The current vintage, the 2006 is benchmark Giorgio. A food-friendly wine – his wife Simonetta is one of the best known winelands cooks in the true Italian style. There is an almost marine kelp minerality which races along with zippy acidity, full flavoured, utterly yummy. His eponymous red is worth a whirl too. And don't forget the fabulous dalla Cia Grappa.

dalla Cia Sauvignon Blanc, 2006, Stellenbosch

DALLA CIA

SAUVIGNON BLANC
2006

WINE OF ORIGIN STELLENBOSCH

PRODUCT OF THE REPUBLIC OF SOUTH AFRICA

" reminds me of eating sun warm mulberries off the farmyard tree as a boy, leaving purple splashes on my shirt "

R55
Durbanville Hills Merlot, 2005, Durbanville

The hills of Durbanville are where I grew up on a wine farm. Now the hi- tech Durbanville Hills cellar processes the grapes of 7 Durbanville growers. Their Merlot is one of my great favourites. There are herbal, fynbos notes on the berried, blood plum nose. Minty eucalyptussy, mineral and gamey undertones support a warm mulberry mouthful which reminds me of eating sun warm mulberries off the farmyard tree as a boy, leaving purple splashes on my shirt.

"The Merlot is one of my faves"

Ernst and Gwenda Gous and their winemaker daughter, Ezanne run a little family business whose net spreads wide into Europe, so popular are their wines. Well settled at Koelenhof Cellars, they use grapes from their own farm and from contracted vineyards to make some stunners. The Merlot is one of my faves, nuances of star anise – a traditional old Cape spice by the way – and a minerally fruit savouriness with blood plums and mulberries wrap around a highish alcohol and give a wine which goes on and on and.....

Ernst & Co Merlot, 2005, Stellenbosch

R65

The house of Fleur du Cap is a label to look for, especially the Unfiltered range. This little bottle of sweetness is just the ticket for the end of a meal – or perhaps the beginning with a good paté or if you are indulging in some foie gras. It's not as sweet as most botrytis affected wines, has the aromatic smells of Gewürztraminer, the tastes of apricots and orange marmalade and a spike of acidity which lifts it into the realms of seriousness.

Fleur du Cap Noble Late Harvest, 2004, Stellenbosch

R90

R62

Hidden Valley Land's End Sauvignon Blanc, 2006, Stellenbosch

Chris Kelly is making some interesting wines in his modern hi-tech cellar so high up on the Helderberg you almost need an oxygen mask. Lovely Stellenbosch wines – especially the Pinotage from ancient Devon Valley vines – and some amazing stuff from down south – Elim-Agulhas way, the provenance of the grapes for this one. Had a walk through the cellar tasting some Elim reds from the barrel which will blow your socks off when they come on the market. This and the other Hidden Valley wines will keep you way more than happy till then.

R81
Iona Merlot Cabernet Sauvignon, 2004, Elgin

We served some of Andrew Gunn's early Sauvignon Blancs in our restaurant with great success. Now along comes Merlot Cabernet Sauvignon, a fine upright specimen of a minerally Bordeaux-style wine. Bright sparky blackcurrant fruit and warm dusty sun-ripened mulberries, with fynbos herbs all laid on a bed of French oak showing through as vanilla and a bit of smoke. Utterly yummy wine from Elgin – cool wine country not only in temperature.

Gary Jordan went to nursery school with my sister Helen, so I knew him as a little boy. He and Kathy make an enchanting duo in the Cellar and make an enchanting Merlot too. It's a confident wine, yet understated. Great fruit – deep and dark and delicious, fresh of acidity and of perfect ripeness, round and soft. The new and used oak support all the elements and make this such a superb utterly yummo wine. They launched a sensational 'real' Rosé this year – dry and cherry lipstick pink, delicious Shiraz fruit.

Jordan Merlot, 2005, Stellenbosch

R76

Kaapzicht Estate Pinotage, 2003, Stellenbosch

Kaapzicht is the Pinotage I use whenever I do a varietal presentation, it's so true to form. Danie Steytler is one of those humble, modest people who let their great wines speak for themselves. Quite frankly this is simply great wine. Smells to fill your sinuses, ripe sweet purple plums, fat mulberries and fresh black cherries; juice running down your chin, enough soft ripe tannin and oaky vanilla to show their presence and back up the fruit.

R68

> ## It's steal at the price – such over-delivering at this price is almost criminal

Kango Cabernet Sauvignon Merlot Shiraz 2006

Gold medallist at the 2007 Swiss International Airlines Wine Awards. I tasted this wine recently with Flip and Caren Smith – he's the winemaker of the Kango Winery in Oudtshoorn. So yummy and already drinking amazingly well – lots of rustic berries and red-black ripe plums. It's a steal at the price – such over-delivering at this price is almost criminal. They're good people too if you're passing through Oudtshoorn – they're in Van der Riet Street. Excellent Kango Swartberg Reserve Shiraz 2005 made by Flip from a very high vineyard on the Swartberg.

R33

> **elegant and surrounded by a frilled tutu of fruit of the refreshing kind; lovely long aftertaste**

R59

Neil Ellis Groenekloof Sauvignon Blanc, 2006, Darling

Neil Ellis was the earliest negoçiant in the Cape and he makes the yummiest wines, Cabernet Sauvignon, Shiraz, Chardonnay and Pinotage. All his entries in the Platter guide are in red. This sublime Sauvignon from Neil's vineyards along the west coast has a steely core holding up a perfectly balanced prima ballerina, delicate, elegant and surrounded by a frilled tutu of fruit of the refreshing kind; lovely long aftertaste. Easy to get into too – it's screwcapped.

Mons Fino Sherry, Paarl

R58

While not strictly a wine, I must include this Monis Fino Sherry in this book. Since visiting the Sandeman Sherry bodega in Jerez in the dying years of the swinging 60s I have been mad for Sherry. It is such an under-rated drink and served cold before a meal is the perfect appetite 'awakener'. The colour of a delicate piece of amber, nose and palate showing all the wondrous nuttiness given to it by the barrel aging covered in the milky clouds of flor yeast, it's soft and dry and utterly yummy.

R72

Desiderius Pongrácz was a legend in the Cape winelands and the legend lives on in this ever-so-popular brut and bubbly wine made by the Methode Cap Classique, emulating the processes used in Champagne for their eponymous sparkler. In amongst the bubbles which rush upwards in the glass you'll find some delicious appley flavours overlaid by toasted almond brioche from the long lie on the lees. It varies occasionally, but then it is a fermented in a bottle so a little variation for me adds to the charm.

Pongrácz, NV, Stellenbosch

"This one comes out of the glass like a glove of a champion boxer"

R60
Ross Gower Sauvignon Blanc, 2006, Elgin

Ross Gower is a gentle, laid-back soul, making huge vinous statements in Elgin after his great successes in Constantia. This one comes out of the glass like a glove of a champion boxer, all the pyrazines in place and ready to tackle almost any food put before it. Smells and tastes of green asparagus and tinned peas and is that eucalyptus? Excellent Pinot Noir Brut by Ross too – the first MCC from Elgin – which is pink like Nicole Kidman's blushing cheek. Just gives the flavour of every berry from straw to blue, and cherries too.

R53
Ses'fikile – Cabernet Franc Cabernet Sauvignon, 2005

Ses'fikile is a wine company made up of three ladies, who, in the translation of the name, have '*arrived in style*'. These three Khayelitsha teachers burst on to the wine scene last year with a range of eight wines made for them by Bruce Jack of Flagstone Winery in Somerset West. Ses'fikile Cabernet Franc Cabernet Sauvignon has the mushroomy, freshly turned earth flavours of the Franc and the broad red and black berries of the Sauvignon. Quite grippy tannins and very food friendly.

Pioneering wine this. The Cape's first champagne-style wine was made from Chenin Blanc by the late Frans Malan on Simonsig Estate almost 40 years ago. Today it's pure Chardonnay and Pinot Noir and the style is called Methode Cap Classique. Having had cellar tours with Frans in the 1970s while he proudly displayed the riddling method of the bottles during second fermentation, I am mildly biased. This is mid-week celebration wine in our house. Now made by Johan Malan, Frans's son, some of the wine is oak barreled to add a bit of breadth to the palate. It's apple pie with almond pastry, lemon curd with finest racy, zippy, zesty little bubbles.

Simonsig Kaapse Vonkel, 2005, Stellenbosch

R65

Spier Private Collection Chenin Blanc, 2006, Stellenbosch

R75

Spier has a knack of turning out good Chenin – Eleonor Visser, their little slip of a maker of white wine has walked away as the WINE Magazine Chenin Blanc Challenge winner. Bags of the most elegant of fruit – melon, white-fleshed peaches and orange and pink grapefruit skin oil singing a gentle chorus throughout; mineral edges and juice-making acidity make this a real wine experience. The 15 months spent in excellent quality French oak have polished the wine without overpowering the heroic fruit. Good ager too if you can bear to lie it down.

R35
Stormhoek Pinotage, 2005, Wellington

Graham Knox's Stormhoek Pino is the wine which not only won a major trophy in London last year, but has also had its popularity laid at the screen of a very successful blog – go look at www.stormhoek.com. *Stormhoek, because the wine business needs a kick in the pants.* And it gets one – this wine is flying off the shelves in the UK, flying the South African Pinotage flag, and no wonder: all that chunky, sappy, purple, plummy fruit, soft and velvety with sweet American oak vanilla and toast and coffee and chocolate. Yum and Yum and Yum again.

> **Juicy ripe melon and granadilla, minerally like a good white Bordeaux**

R70
Vergelegen Sauvignon Blanc, 2006, Stellenbosch

Andre van Rensburg does wonderful stuff in his eyrie on Vergelegen and each year needs a truck to carry off his trophies at the Old Mutual Trophy Wine Show (run with such precision and humour by Michael Fridjhon). Andre blends in a splash of Semillon and oaks a portion of the wine to fill out the palate. Juicy ripe melon and granadilla, minerally like a good white Bordeaux. Fresh too, a perfect food wine – can almost taste the mussels.

R50

Jeff Grier has been making simply sublime and great value bubbles for a long time on Villiera. The Tradition Brut has some Pinotage blended in with the Chardonnay, Pinot Noir and Pinot Meuniére, the classical Champagne grapes. Soft on the palate, exciting fine bubbles, palate cleansing and very food friendly. The Rosé Brut is a winner with the pink coming from mainly Pinotage. Racy acidity, nice dry finish.

Villiera Tradition Brut, NV, Stellenbosch

Welgegund Carignan, 2004, Wellington

R45

The only bottled Carignan in the Cape for some time and punted with almost religious fervour by Alex Camerer, owner of Welgegund. Carignan, a southern French grape, does well in the warm climes of Wellington. Rhone sister varietal Shiraz – splash of – is blended in to add to the spectrum of flavours. Good colour though it tends to be lighter than most reds. Warm mulberry and other berry flavours. Pop it in an ice bucket half an hour before lunch – really yummy with cold rare beef and gentle whole grain mustard.

Out to impress is all about, well, impressing. Boss or mother in law coming to dinner? Wine geek friend you want to bowl over? And they're not top price wines necessarily, just unusual ones.

> **Barbera grapes are high in acidity which is carried over into the wine with soft gentle tannins**

R55

Altydgedacht Barbera, 2003, Durbanville

Jean Parker farmed along our borders when I was a boy, and now sons John and Oliver make some stunning wines. This is the pioneer Barbera, great grape of Piedmont – in South Africa. Barbera grapes are high in acidity, carried over into the wine with soft gentle tannins. Deep purplish black, it has smells and tastes of ripe red fruit, redcurrants and plums in a wine just so different from the usual suspects. Toasty vanilla smoke from the French and American Oak aging add fruit flavours.

R60
Bon Cap Organic Cabernet Sauvignon, 2006, Robertson

The soils in the vineyards of the organically farmed Bon Cap are like fruit cake. Roelf and Michelle du Preez hold their farm in trust for future generations and care for it with passion. Hugely successful, their cellar is empty of stock. Roelf crafts this fruit burst of a wine, which is laden with local medals and awards, as well as those of Biofach, the big German Organic Fair. Soft, rich velvet textured fruit in concentration with savoury notes of Parma ham. This is a real stonker.

R115

Cape Point Sauvignon Blanc, 2007, Noordhoek

Duncan Savage needs no more laurel wreaths; he has them all from the Old Mutual Trophy Wine Show 2007. His Sauvignon Blanc is a real cool customer. Very French, very Loire. Citrus present as lime squirt and naartjie peel, lovely minerals sucked up from the Cape Point soil. Concentration of flavours, rich and full. Get the cork out fast – this one will impress even the most hard core winos.

R85
Cederberg Cabernet Sauvignon, 2004, Cederberg

This is mind-blowing stuff. Extreme farming in the Cederberg with the country's highest vineyards. Packed with spicy black fruit, blackcurrants and blueberries. Soft sweet ripe smooth tannins – brilliant package of wine with lovely new French oak shining through the fruit. 2005's a stunner too. David Niewoudt's Bukettraube is a dream, honey and flowers and spice, great wine for oriental food, cuts like rapier through all that sweet chili and honey!

"control from vine to bottle"

R89
Cordoba Merlot,
2002, Stellenbosch

Chris Keet has his hands on the vineyards of Cordoba
– a great advantage when you are producing serious
wine as he does, control from vine to bottle. Apart
from a blast of red and black berries and cherries,
you'll find caffe latte notes with dark 70% chocolate
as well as some eucalyptus and mint which I find so
enchanting in some Western Australian and Cape reds.

> **Rianie Strydom has a way with wine – especially reds**

Dombeya Amalgam, 2004, Stellenbosch

R60

Rianie Strydom has a way with wine – especially reds. This amalgam of flavours – it's a Cabernet Sauvignon, Shiraz and Merlot blend – shows dark black Morello cherries with the blackcurrant of a good Bordeaux winking away in the background through some chunky, yet accessible tannins and all on a firm platform of oak from Rianies use of second and third fill barrels. Named Dombeya, it is the entry level wine of Haskell Vineyards – a name to watch out for in future – Rianie's there.

R52

Groote Post Sauvignon Blanc, 2006, Darling

Groote Post was a dairy farm where Peter Pentz won international prizes for his cows; now it's all covered in vines. This former home of famous South African cookery writer, Hildagonda Duckitt, is now the home of some fine wines. Darling, and the effect the cold Atlantic Ocean has on its vineyards, is prime Sauvignon Blanc country.

Packed with the flavours of crisp apple and green pepper and dusty fynbos herbaceousness, you'll find slices of fresh white fleshed fig and limesquirt adding a twist at the end of this crisp little number.

R76
Hermanuspietersfontein
Kleinboet, 2005, Hermanus

Bartho Eksteen makes wines with wonderful 'mouth feel' and no exception is Kleinboet, all five Bordeaux varieties, which cries out for roasted or grilled red meat – there must be caramelly bits to meet this soft gentle mouthful of richness of berries and oak (21 months in small barrels) and spice and minerals. While Hermanuspietersfontein must be the longest name for a cellar in South Africa, it's a short run to your local or to Hermanus to load a couple of cases of this into your boot.

If you love wine, you have to drink this wine at least once in your lifetime

R140
Kanonkop Pinotage, 2004, Stellenbosch

Think Pinotage, and Pavlovian bells ring out Kanonkop. Johann and Paul Krige caretake the Estate of their late grandfather, politico and red wine connoisseur, Paul Sauer (also their eponymous flagship red). Pinotage fruit at its purest yet loudest and clearest, new French Oak barrels adding their supportive flavours and balancing out the whopping nearly 15% alcohol. Restrained like an elegant finely tuned racehorse before a race. If you love wine, you have to drink this wine at least once in your lifetime. And take your hat off while you are doing it. And kneel. And tug your forelock.

Muratie Pinot Noir, 2005, Stellenbosch

R115

I have known the only two owners of Muratie in my lifetime, Annemie Canitz whose father bought it in 1926 and the Melck Family. Ronnie, the *pater familias* is a legend in his own lunchtime (to plagiarise someone, I can't remember who), who bought it back from Annemie after the Estate had been out of the ownership of his family for over 100 years. Pinot Noir has been part of Muratie for ages. This Melck wine is strawberry coloured with white heart cherries and raspberries side by side with mushrooms and forest floor smells and tastes. Lovely ripe tannins wrapping round the fruit and the oak present in the wine as a delicate thread from nose to tail.

R150

Oak Valley Pinot Noir, 2006, Elgin

When Anthony and Madeleine Rawbone Viljoen produced their first
Oak Valley Sauvignon Blanc, the local wine world was muttering,
"Is this the finest Cape Sauvignon yet?" It's a great wine. But what endeared
me most to their Pinot Noir was that I drank it with some fabulous Cepe
mushrooms freshly gathered from under the oaks at Oak Valley. What a
combo! The forest floor fresh mushroom smells combined with classical
Burgundy cherries and strawberries and new French oak gently humming
in the background – clever use of classy oak by winemaker Pieter Visser.

'Pinot Noir and cepes What a combo!'

R89

Danie Truter's Onderkloof sits below Sir Lowry's Pass on the eastern slopes of the Schaapenberg. That's the little bump in the Helderberg bowl that gathers about itself cooling mists, lowering vineyard temperatures in the ripening time. His Cabernet Sauvignon, long one of my favourites, shows such elegance and lots of fruit, mainly blackcurrant, crème de cassis and toasted, restrained oak. Danie imports barrels from Tonnellerie Rousseau, a small family cooperage and prefers their House Blend barrels which are a mix of several forests and are medium toasted, which preserves the fruit and terroir aromas of the Cabernet.

Onderkloof Cabernet Sauvignon, 2002, Stellenbosch

Paul Cluver Gewürztraminer, 2006, Elgin

"**Yummy stuff**"

R45

Gewürztraminer, one of the most underrated white varietals in South Africa (the other being the true Riesling), reveals its colours in the Paul Cluver bottle. Elegant, tropical flowers like frangipani and rose petals precede white fleshed peaches and mangosteen fruit. The brilliant cape gooseberry acidity mask the little bit of residual sugar – it's really almost classically dry. Gently spiced Indian or Vietnamese food just scream for this wine as does a chunky smoked snoek paté on Melba toast.

R110

This bag of sappy chunky fruit of the cassis kind is beautifully brushed by excellent French oak and has undertones of delicious mint and blue gum. Niel Bester proves he is no slouch with the other labels, red and white, from this beautiful Estate in Simondium.

Plaisir de Merle Cabernet Sauvignon, 2003, Simondium

Really dignified, almost hand made, like a perfectly blown glass, wine of the deepest and broadest complexity. Stunningly balanced, the brilliant natural sappiness of the fruit beautifully integrated with its acidity, the excellent oak and each of the three grapes which make up the blend contributing its own virtues. Blackcurrant and blueberry from the Cabernet, blood plums and raspberries from the Merlot and fine Italian leather and spice tones of the Shiraz. Part matured in open top Demi-Muids – a 600-litre oak vat typical of those used in the Rhone Valley.

R175

Radford Dale Gravity, 2005, Stellenbosch

> **The bottle looks like a Mexican Army General with all its medals** "

**R75
Raka Quinary,
2003, Klein Rivier**

Piet Dreyer is a rough man of the sea, a chokka fisherman who keeps company with the best in Bordeaux, with a slew of medals hanging from his neck from Michelangelo, SAA and Veritas for his wines. The bottle looks like a Mexican Army General with all his medals. The Quinary (Latin for *of five*) blends the Bordeaux grapes from Piet's farm near Stanford and east of Hermanus, into a harmonious mélange of ripe berries and accessible tannins with cassis and "just a whiff of cigars".

R70
Ridgeback Merlot Cabernet Franc, 2004, Paarl

Vernon Cole has created a bit of paradise round the back of Paarl Mountain. Superb vineyards watched over by über Californian consultant Phil Freese and cellar under Catherine Marshall, arch Oeno-Francophile. In this blend red black plums poached with cinnamon stick from the Merlot and freshly turned sod and blackberry from the Cabernet Franc create a wine of generous proportions. Using only a small percentage of new oak, the wood has given its character to the wine while allowing the fruit to perform wondrously. The Shiraz from Ridgeback is a legend in its own time – previous winner of the Paarl Shiraz Challenge.

Rupert & Rothschild Baron Edmond, Simondium, 2002

Rupert and Rothschild make a habit of really great wine. Fruit, fruit, fruit – savoury rather than sweet and a tremendous amount of guts. Ripe, ripe tannins and grandstanding wood from twenty or so months in new French Oak. Schalk Willem Joubert, the wine maker and his team sort and de-stem by hand and then ferment their reds in 500-litre oak barrels. Second label Cab Merlot blend, the Classique, is also an excellent offering.

R198

R55

Stellar Organics Heaven on Earth, 2006, Klawer

Dudley Wilson is a dedicated organic wine producer. Up in Klawer disease is minimal and water is pure. This is a classically produced wine – a *Vin de Thé Rouge*. The Muscat of Alexandria grapes are laid out in the sun on organic rooibos tea to dehydrate and concentrate. Before pressing they are crushed and destemmed and allowed to lie on their own skins. Fermentation takes place in barrels, adding some oak and vanilla flavours. This results in this rich essence of honey with sun ripened apricots and roasted pineapple, brilliantly balanced. Really yummy wines from this cellar, excellent reds and sparky zippy whites.

> **This is a benchmark Shiraz from Guy Webber – the quiet confident winemaker**

R160
Stellenzicht Vineyards Syrah, 2001, Stellenbosch

Long time on of my favourites, it's won almost every single accolade going. What more does one need to recommend a wine with all this third party endorsement? This is a benchmark Shiraz from Guy Webber, the quiet, confident winemaker. Sappy and somewhat smoky fruit, fine Italian leather and savoury pepper. Such an elegant number which comes from a vineyard called Plum Pudding Hill, says it all.

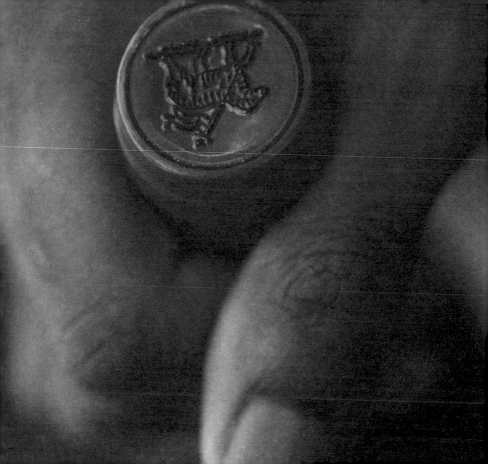

R70

The name Sterhuis – meaning "star house", dates to the 17th Century, when early Capetonians mistook the light shining in the farmhouse high on the distant Bottelary Hills in the East for Venus, the evening star. From his steep vineyards, Johan Kruger achieves full blast berry fruits with spiced mulberry and brushes it with half new, half previous fill French oak, all hung around a core of restrained elegance and style. Winner of the Diners Club Young Winemaker of the Year 2005 for his Sterhuis Chardonnay. Motto? No easy journey from the earth to the stars.

Sterhuis Merlot, 2004, Stellenbosch

R112
Vins d' Orrance Chardonnay, 2005, Constantia

Gentle giant Christophe Durand comes from a family of Normandy Calvados makers, has the build of a rugby forward, and the ability to produce wines of great elegance and the gentlest touch. He makes only this Chardonnay using Constantia grapes and a Shiraz from Stellenbosch grapes, matured in his own oak barrels – he is an importer of barrels from two family cooperages in France. This is as elegant a wine as if it was a top Paris fashion piece. Great mouthfeel, delicate yet a brilliant essence of Chardonnay flavour, buttery toasted brioche and lime squeeze.

R65
Vriesenhof Enthopio, 2003, Stellenbosch

Jan Boland Coetzee will be in shorts and short sleeved shirt when all about him are in anoraks: I can't recall ever seeing him in a coat or jersey! His wines are like him, kind, generous, ready smile and a good feeling having seen him. This one is heavy on be-muscled Pinotage with big soft accessible tannins and juicy, juicy berries – black and straw – interesting mushroomy flavours coming I suspect off the Cabernet Franc component. This is a wine to drink with marinated roasted venison.

R140

Warwick Cabernet Franc, 2005, Stellenbosch

Norma Ratcliffe's early examples of this wine set a trend which has
continued in the hands of Louis Nel who now makes the wines at Warwick.
Once you are able to get your eyes off the deep ruby brilliance and you get
your nose into the glass, there is creamy milk chocolate with almonds,
on tasting the fruit is ripe and almost chewy. Good coffee, dark cherry
and licorice lurk to give a long tail of fabulous and lingering sweetness.

" **Norma Ratcliffe's early examples
of this wine set a trend** "

Blond Schalk Burger, the Springbok No 6 is a big fella, his eponymous father is positively huge. 2005 was Welbedacht's maiden vintage of Pinotage, which, Schalk Snr says, "displays a seductive elegance more reminiscent of New World Pinot Noir than old-school Pinotage". Powerful red berries and rubbed tomato leaves accompany some flowers on the nose, while the oak gives classical coconut and vanilla sweetness to the generous fruit. There is coffee too and spices like cinnamon feathers, black pepper and cloves. Its huge alcohol makes it a food wine and it can take big flavours.

Welbedacht Barrique Select Pinotage, 2005, Wellington

R65

And finally *Splashing out* will offer some utterly delicious wonderpieces for which you might have to pay the price, but the joy will be unconfined.

R63

Ataraxia Sauvignon Blanc, 2007, Hermanus

Imagine taking two flint stones and cracking them together. Add to the flinty
charge some whiffs of green – like grass cuttings, pepper and herbal fynbos
flowers, add a sea kelp minerality, some poached cape gooseberry acidity,
squeezings of sweet lime and grapefruit skin oil. Ataraxia! Wine Spectator
loved it this year 92/100. I just loved it – you will too.

> **I just loved it – you will too.**

The Maverick was Bernard Podlashuk owner of Bellingham in the middle to latter part of last century. This is benchmark Viognier, ripe nectarines and spicy acidy apricot compote full and rich with the oak ever present. This goes well with cured meats like Parma ham, mild salami as well as the more obvious chopstick food. There are other wines in this range – the Chenin showing particularly well.

Bellingham The Maverick Viognier, 2005, Franschhoek

R72

R120

There's a chap in Greyton called Richard von Gesau who makes a dark chocolate mixed with chai tea spices. It could be a solid form of this wine, and the name is perfect – The Chocolate Block. But other flavours lurk here too. When you take a raft of grape varieties you get breadth of flavour, aromatics from Viognier, dusty spicy sweet fruit from the Cinsaut, Grenache and Shiraz and the elegance and structure of the Cabernet. Popular stuff this, try and land a bottle.

Boekenhoutskloof The Chocolate Block, 2006, Franschhoek

R130
Bouchard Finlayson
Hannibal,
2004, Hermanus

Peter Finlayson in this wine
combines France (Pinot Noir),
Italy (Sangiovese and Nebbiolo),
and Africa – Hannibal on African
elephants crossing from France
to Italy! Stature and elegance
and packing a punch in terms of
fruit and flavour. Brushed up with
the oak it makes for something
unique. Peter has an ability to
create a mouthfeel in his wines
which makes them so deeply
delicious. At the other end of the
scale is the white, Blanc de Mer
the 2007 version of which
is knockout fish wine.

> **"You feel good when you drink this wine, like you do when you meet Cathy."**

R89

Catherine Marshall
Syrah, 2004, Paarl

Cathy Marshall loves and identifies with the wines of France, so her wines have that elegance and dignity rather than full frontal fruit attack. So you get wondrous fruit in this multi-layered Syrah, deep and dark ruby fruit, centred round a savoury almost meaty, gamey mineraliness and wrapped in oak which is elegantly present in a most understated way. You feel good when you drink this wine, like you do when you meet Cathy.

R90

Constantia Glen Sauvignon Blanc, 2006, Constantia

Some of the greatest Cape Sauvignon Blancs come from Constantia. It almost goes without saying that Constantia Glen should be a shining star too. Only in its second vintage and brilliant it is, finding itself on the lists of some of the best of London restaurants. Flavour breadth that goes over the horizon, soft acidity like squashed, ripe, sun warmed, apricots, other tropical fruits and crisp chunky green melon and a seaweed sweet-saltiness which I find utterly appealing. Karl Lambour has more excitement up his sleeve – can a red be far behind?

> Only in its second vintage and brilliant it is, finding itself on the lists of some of the best of London restaurants

They call this *The People's Pinotage*, a cult wine if ever there was one. David Sonnenberg and his team at Diemersfontein are on an unstoppable train. I know at least one person who should be hospitalized to help him over his addiction to this wine. Coffee and chocolate brought out by well toasted spicy oak and great frais des bois fruit to cope with it, makes this an easy quaffer of note. You can happily drink it on its own it's so soft and appealing.

R67
Diemersfontein Pinotage, 2006, Wellington

Grangehurst Cabernet Sauvignon Merlot, 2001, Stellenbosch

> **This man makes serious wine**

R120

Jeremy Walker's reds come from the birthplace of great red wines, the slopes of the Helderberg. I love the fruit in this wine, it has the blackcurrant cassis flavour with some lifted raspberry one expects from a Bordeaux style blend. Cedar and pencil shavings and fynbos smells are there too. The wine though ready to drink once released from Grangehurst, will give great joy in years to come if you can bear to keep it that long. This man makes serious wine.

R275

Klein Constantia Vin de Constance, 2002, Constantia

I once tasted an early 19th century version of this wine with the Jooste family who own Klein Constantia. How could one not be moved by a wine written about by Jane Eyre, Charles Dickens and Baudelaire, drunk by the crowned heads of Europe and called for by Napoleon in exile on St Helena? This 21st century version is one Cape wine we need to take seriously, for it is an icon. It's elegantly packaged in a beautiful hand-blown look bottle with a simple label. The Muscat de Frontignac simply bulges with flowers and fruit and raisins and soft citrus skin oil and gentle acidity. Doesn't need botrytis – it's just alive with flavour.

Visiting this vineyard where things have been done to such perfection by Gerard and Libby de Villiers, you can feel it is loved, for *Kleinood* is Afrikaans for a treasure. A small perfect vineyard planted by Aidan Morton, a small perfect cellar designed by Gerard with some lovely Libby touches of old Indian windows and doors in a quintessentially Cape building and set in a tranquil rose and lavender filled garden. The Tamboerskloof Syrah 2004 has a single thread running through it from nose to aftertaste with all the components beautifully integrated. Oak, raspberries, fine Cuban cigars, violets, violets, violets and spice on the nose. Complex well-balanced mouthfeel with berries and almonds on the aftertaste.

Kleinood Tamboerskloof Syrah, 2005, Stellenbosch

R85

R68
La Motte Pierneef Collection Sauvignon Blanc, 2007, Franschhoek

The premier white wine of La Motte Estate – the Pierneef Collection – a sensational Sauvignon Blanc from their own organically grown vineyards down Walker Bay way. La Motte is one of the Rupert family's show-piece estates in Franschhoek. The labels of the collection are illustrated with lino cuts from the Rupert collection of Pierneefs. Flinty *rain-on-soil* aromas followed by overt tropical fruit, tangy granadilla and aromatic mango flavours. Very sparky acidity perfectly balanced with citrus – citron preserve and shaddock. Big serious wine.

Le Riche Cabernet Sauvignon, 2003, Stellenbosch

> **The most perfect balance of acidity, oak, savoury minerals, soft tannins and blackcurrants**

R100

One of my most favourite Cabernet Sauvignons made by one of the most unassuming of winemakers, Etienne le Riche who has such a confident delicacy of touch with his wines. This is a wine of great stature and elegance and has a deep core of rich black fruit – cassis and blackberries. The most perfect balance of acidity, oak, savoury minerals, soft tannins and blackcurrants. The Reserve is a step up. Soft utterly delicious Merlot too.

R120

Mark Lindhorst worked for me as an accountancy student in 1975; he has made as much of a success of his second career as he did with his first. Shiraz is Mark and Belinda Lindhorst's Wine. And this is an consummate example of New World Shiraz from which Cathy Marshall as winemaker coaxes subtle spice and vanilla from the oak in counterpoint to the rich chunky fruit and the ripe tannins. Try the tongue in cheek named Statement for a serious, well, statement of what Lindhorst is all about.

Lindhorst Shiraz, 2005, Paarl

R250
Meerendal Heritage Collection Pinotage, 2005, Durbanville

In 1952 former owner Kosie Starke planted the vineyard for this wine. Deeply coloured, a sort of royal purple, the wine has brilliant berry and wild bramble whiffs, fat dark cherries and blood plums and the spiciness of cinnamon and vanilla like a rich Christmas pudding. Lovely big broad sweeps of flavour on the palate with soft, yet oh so necessary tannins and just the most superb use of oak. Still a baby but with its complexity and fullness of flavour, there's potential for development to celebrate the vineyards 75th birthday – if you can wait that long.

R126
Meerlust Chardonnay, 2004, Stellenbosch

Chris Williams ferments half the Meerlust
Chardonnay in oak barrels and the balance in
tanks which, when blended together produces a
Chardonnay retaining some of its youthful freshness.
There is an enchanting presence of citrus in the shape
of the finest orange marmalade and the oak is there
from the first sniff to after the last swallow in a single
thread. It fills your mouth with a richness of texture,
a lusciousness of fruit and a minerality which can
only come from rich and ancient soils.

Meinert Synchronicity, 2004, Stellenbosch

R154

Martin Meinert not only produces one of the Cape's most lauded Chenins in the FMC – the Forrester Meinert Chenin – he does it here with this totally sublime red. Fat fruit washing around, spiced with 'sweet' spices and vanilla – brilliantly structured tannins and just the most perfect use of new French oak. This wine says 'respect me'.

A happy invasion of the Cape by the French. Anne Cointreau is one perfectionist lady. Over the years of her ownership the farm has been replanted, a most beautiful cellar built, excellent restaurants and function facilities opened and sublime wine made. The entry level Fantail wines are a fun production with quirky Peacock labels but there's nothing quirky in the bottle. This Première Sélection lies in barrels in the most aesthetically pleasing maturation cellar you'll see in the Cape, you could be in a Chateau in Bordeaux. And the wine reflects it – refined, restrained, elegant and deep in colour, deep berry core, ripe sweet five reds from Bordeaux, superb touch with the oak and quite exceptionally delicious.

Morgenhof Première Sélection, 2001, Stellenbosch

R165

R99
Morgenster Lourens River Valley, 2001, Stellenbosch

Marius Lategan is able to coax every drop of goodness
from his grapes which have drawn up every drop of
goodness from the Morgenster soils. The Cabernet Franc
content adds its fresh turned sod aromas, freshly sliced
mushrooms buzzing around in the smells while the
Merlot provides Tayberry, pomegranate and blood plums,
the oak adding the spice and creamy vanilla. There is
a top of the range red named for the estate Morgenster.
If you haven't tried the olive oil from Morgenster, you
are depriving yourself of a great deal of pleasure.

R205
Raats Cabernet Franc, 2005, Stellenbosch

One of a few Cabernet Francs bottled in the Cape – and it is a perfect one. And displaying all the grape has to offer in terms of its varietal characteristics and maturing possibilities. The darkest of ruby in colour with cranberry edges, there are ripe Agen plums and Morello cherries wrapped in Christmas pudding spiced dark chocolate and the softest silkiest tannins from nose to tail. Such a stunner from one of the real gentlemen of the winelands.

R245

**Using natural yeasts Adi Badenhorst has crafted the most brilliant of
Chardonnays in the Rustenberg 5 Soldiers, the flagship white on this,
one of the oldest estates in the Cape. Wonderful fruit of the overt full frontal
Dolly Parton kind, oak is, as one would expect, all new French. Sublime
stuff. Nuff said.**

Rustenburg 5 Soldiers, 2005, Stellenbosch

Charles Back is a free spirit and his thought processes go way beyond the horizon and way out of the box. The huge international success that is Goats do Roam, the fabulous Fairview Wines, and Spice Route speak volumes about this driven and kind soul. The Malabar – Malabar is a region on the western Indian coast north of Kerala – is deep crimson red in colour with well defined ripe sweet plummy fruit, layered with pimiento and dark chocolate. Rich and with a long lingering aftertaste.

Spice Route Malabar, 2003, Malmesbury

R300

While you may not have heard of Nebbiolo, you would certainly have heard of the great Piedmontese wines from Barolo and Barbaresco which contain this grape. The Steenberg Nebbiolo 2005 is mulberry coloured and the nose is full of soft sundried purple plums and spicy strawberry spoon jam. The fruit presence is delicate with star anise undertones and the previous fill oak showing through. The flavours here are so different – luvverley stuff! They're planting more Nebbiolo vines, so the news is as good for the future as it is tasting back some vintages.

R100

Steenberg Nebbiolo, 2005, Constantia

John Faure is one of the quietest men in the winelands, so laid back he's almost coming up the other side. The wines in his cellar are serious — like him — and tend more to elegant French: restrained, dignified, with great fruit and structure. This is Arnold Schwarzenegger — big and bold, wondrous blackcurrant present in perfect harmony with the spicy oak and the touches of eucalyptus and mint. John uses an interesting combination of French and Russian oak for stature and a touch of American, adding vanilla to the spices already present.

Vergenoegd Cabernet Sauvignon, 2003, Stellenbosch

R90

Waterford Cabernet Sauvignon, 2004, Stellenbosch

Kevin and Heather Arnold are by far the most good looking couple in the winelands. Kevin's wines are pretty sharp too. This one is like a finely trained racehorse aquiver at the starting line. Splashes of Cabernet Franc, Merlot and Malbec add to the flavour spectrum. There is a mass of dark fruit; there are wondrous spices and some dark chocolate showing through from the combination of French and American oak barrels. Tasting a few wines and looking ahead with Kevin recently, this is a place to watch. Because if you don't, something great might escape the cellar door and you might miss it.

R105

Zandvliet Kalkveld Shiraz, 2002, Ashton

R108

Hard to be objective about this wine as I know the place as I planted a vine up on Paul de Wet's Kalkveld on Zandvliet Estate some years ago. Zandvliet, the oldest bottled Shiraz in the Cape – planted in alluvial riverine soil – has younger twin sisters up on the slopes. One appears as American oaked – more easy to drink, softer, mellow and chilled out. This one – the French Oaked version is a more serious sister in a well cut Paris suit. In new French barrels, for 18 months showing fine Italian leather and a touch of smoke on the nose, and such perfection of berries and ripe plums in the mouth.

THE CAPE WINEMAKERS GUILD

Leaders in the art of winemaking
A male dominated group, with Norma Ratcliffe in an honorary role as winemaker emeritus. The Guild was founded in 1982 by eight independent winemakers who shared a vision of creating premium South African wines that would receive benchmark recognition both locally and abroad.

Today the 37 members of the Cape Winemakers Guild share that same vision and, through the exchange of knowledge and the evaluation of top wines from around the world, Guild members have established themselves as leaders in the art of winemaking.

As a means of promoting their wines, the members of the CWG held their first public auction in 1985. Following its early success, the auction, now sponsored by Nedbank, has become a major annual event on the South African wine calendar. The Nedbank CWG Auction is held on the first Saturday of October every year, with a programme of wine-related events taking place during the week prior to the 'big day'. Wines sold at the Nedbank CWG Auction are exclusive. They are produced by the members in small quantities, especially for the Auction, and are not available anywhere else (unless when re-sold by auction buyers).

The Guild also holds a number of exciting public events in the buildup to its annual Auction. With the emphasis firmly placed on 'meeting the winemaker', Guild events are intimate, informal, and interactive.

In 1999, together with its Auction sponsor Nedbank, the Cape Winemakers Guild established the Nedbank CWG Development Trust. Assisting with the social, education and training needs of its own industry workforce, the Trust renders a worthwhile contribution to previously disadvantaged communities.

The Screwpull Corkscrew

While the conventional waiter's friend corkscrew does a good enough job at removing a cork, I am a great fan of the elegantly designed Screwpull Corkscrew and have used one successfully for many years. It was the only corkscrew we used in our restaurants for almost twenty years.

The original self-pulling corkscrew was invented by Screwpull in 1979. Its perfectly shaped Teflon coated screw is designed to glide smoothly through the toughest corks. This amazing corkscrew will ensure that every bottle of wine you open is opened effortlessly.

The Screwpull comes in a variety of models, but the one illustrated on page 130 is perfect.

Also for those of you who need to remove screwcaps, Screwpull have the 4 in 1 – a ducky little contraption which can remove the crown corks off beer bottles, cut the foil off the top of a wine

bottle, remove the cork from a bottle of bubbly and remove
a screwcap with great ease.

Cork or Screw – the grand debate
One of the big debates about wine bottle closures is the cork
versus screwcap or artificial closure.

While my preference is for the screwcap – by far – there are
some positives for cork being a traditional closure. There is of
course the romance of the cellaring. It is not done much today as
most wine is consumed within a day or two of purchase. There is
of course the opening ritual and hearing the cork pop out of the
bottle. This in a way, with all the swirling and sniffing that goes
on, perpetuates the myth that you need a master's degree in
some cryptic subject to understand wine.

The negatives for cork are that you need to have a corkscrew
handy to open a bottle. Imagine going on a picnic and leaving
the corkscrew behind. Cork taint is a major negative, TCA

and fungal infections cause about 6 - 7% of wine to be 'corked' that gives it a musty mouldy wet cardboard – even wet dog – character. TCA (2,4,6-trichloroanisole) is a compound produced by microbes that live in the lenticels of cork bark. Cork can fall apart with age and the bottle needs to be stored horizontally to keep the cork moist thus protecting the seal.

The screwcap on the other hand has a number of plusses. You don't need an implement to open the bottle. It can be stored upright. Importantly, the screwcap is known to retain the wonderful fresh fruit aromas and tastes as the wine ages. And most importantly it makes wine accessible to all by removing the elitism and mythology from wine.

Some say that the screwcap cheapens the image of wine and that all the romance is gone. For me that is simply furthering the smoke and mirrors and large scale bull that goes on about wine. Australia and New Zealand are particularly gung-ho about screwcaps.

Synthetic closures – euphemism for plastic corks – are used in Cape wines and the el cheapo ones are best known for breaking corkscrews.

For me the perfect synthetic closure is the Guala seal pioneered in this country by Giorgio dalla Cia for his eponymous wines. Soft, easy to remove and easy to get back in if you want to return a bottle to the fridge – not that this happens often in our house!

Food and wine matching or pairing

Yet another way for the wine industry to create another mysterious science to the exclusion of the wine-loving public.

You can't change the wine so you need to find a food to match it.

In spite of the plethora of Wine and Cheese parties that were held in years past, I don't believe that wine and cheese really go together that well. Sure there are some wines that are fabulous with cheese; some of the fortifieds like hanepoot or jerepigo go well with the lovely nutty matured cheddars for example. And do regard sherry as a wine – it goes brilliantly with a cheese like a good local blue from Fairview or indeed Stilton. And while we're about it, Sake is a fabulous wine to match with cheese.

The old story of white with white and red with red has also fortunately suffered the fate of fenestration and it is now popular to drink a chilled, fruity young Pinotage with seared tuna or indeed a wonderfully buttery, oaked chardonnay with roast leg of pork.

The greater reds like Cabernet Sauvignon, Pinotage, Merlot and Shiraz go so well with grilled, roasted or barbecued meats. The whites – particularly with softer oaked Chardonnays match chicken and turkey while a crisp Sauvignon Blanc – the favoured varietal in South Africa – cries out for grilled and particularly pan-fried fish, either sea – or freshwater.

The Times of India recently published an article in which they extolled the virtues of red wine with curry rather than the spicy whites like Gewürz and Riesling have been punted previously. Chenin Blanc is great with the softer Thai foods.

The sweeter more grapey wines tend to go well with curries, though I think I would choose a good Cobra Beer above all else in a curry shop!

The best way to master this is simply to experiment to see what works best for you.

WINE COMPETITIONS

Wine Competitions are fraught with all sorts of pros and cons and are a never ending debate.

My favourite competition is the Old Mutual Trophy Wine Show which is usually held in the middle of the year. Michael Fridjhon who runs the competition in conjunction with Wine Magazine always ensures that there are at least two recognised international wine judges present, with a band of locals who know what they are up to. Look out for the stickers on bottles.

Wine Magazine also runs three challenges, The Chenin Blanc Challenge, sponsored by First National Bank, The Cap Classique Challenge, sponsored by Amorim the Portuguese cork suppliers and The Shiraz Challenge sponsored by Pick 'n Pay. Local panels under the Chairmanship of Michael Fridjhon judge these challenges. Public wine tastings give the wine drinker a chance to taste some of the top wines.

The Swiss International Air Lines Wine Awards which are run in conjunction with the Cape Town Gourmet Festival in May each year has well known wine guru, Robert Joseph as its chairman. Chris Murphy, who buys wine for Marks and Spencer identified a need in the South African wine industry to invite an international jury to judge its wines. Judges come from Europe, the USA, UK and Asia and since its inception there has been increasing support for the competition from local producers. The competition is now considered one of the top wine contests in South Africa.

The Michelangelo International Wine Awards was created in 1997 by Lorraine Immelman, wine lover and marketing consultant, when she identified a need in the wine industry for the creation of an international wine competition for South Africa: an international and local jury judging local wines. Since its inception there has been increasing support for the competition among local producers and today it is considered one of the top wine contests in South Africa.

ABSA Top Ten Pinotage Awards takes place each year – well worth watching out for those results as a guide to the Pinotages for which you should be looking out on the shelves.

The SA Terroir Awards was one competition about which I was very sceptical until I attended the Awards lunch this year. While I am still not sure that I could tell a Stellenbosch Merlot from a Durbanville one in a blind tasting, I was very impressed with the quality of wine which was presented at the lunch.

Many South African producers enter their wines for Chardonnay du Monde, Syrah du Monde, International Wine Challenge and The International Wine & Spirit Competition – which is now in its 38th year – and aims to promote the quality and excellence of the world's best wines, spirits and liqueurs.

While they are not competitions, Winex (held in Cape Town and Johannesburg) each year and the Juliet Cullinan Wine Awards – tastings in Cape Town, Durban and Johannesburg

– also offer a brilliant opportunity for the public to taste a vast array of local wines.

The Diners Club Winemaker and Young Winemaker of the Year Awards should be taken seriously too and the wines which get up near the top each year are some of the best available. Each year a different variety or style of wine is chosen as the subject of the competition.

Though not actually a wine competition, the Diners Club Wine List of the Year Awards honours restaurants which go the extra mile in the preparation of their wine lists. The award winners, which can be found on the Diners Club Web Site www.dinersclub.co.za, should be sought out if you want a good drop with your meal.

Capetonians should look out for the Caroline's Red and White Wine Reviews and the Wine Concepts Super Sauvignons tasting held in August.

WHERE DO I GET INFORMATION ABOUT WINE?

Contact details of all the producers in this book can be found in the Wine Magazine publications and the John Platter South African Wines Guide.

Apart from an excellent monthly magazine, WINE Magazine, also produces an annual called Icons which is published to coincide with the Old Mutual Trophy Wine Show in June.

Other WINE Magazine publications which are a mine of information are the Pocket Guide to Wines & Cellars of South Africa, and the Best Value Wine Guide which offers almost 500 wines at under R40.

The weekly email newsletter Gulp is worth subscribing to as the Webmaster for Wine Magazine Christian Eedes has an unusual take on wine.

Cassie du Plessis edits two wine orientated magazines called Wineland and Fynproe, which is an Afrikaans wine and lifestyle magazine.

Read the wine columns in magazines and your local newspaper.

WHERE CAN I BUY WINES?

Pick 'n Pay, the national supermarket group offers in its supermarkets, Family Supermarkets and Hypermarkets the broadest of ranges at quite exceptional prices. Other supermarkets chains which have a smaller share of the market are worth visiting, particularly when they offer specials.

Wine producers are happy to deliver wines to almost anywhere in South Africa and in some cases, will send wine off shore at a price!

SPECIALIST WINE SHOPS
IN THE MAJOR CENTRES ARE:

CAPE TOWN
Wine Concepts
Started by Mike Bampfield Duggan and Murray Giggins, Wine Concepts are real wine specialists. They will offer the complete wine service from stocking up your cellar on a monthly basis according to your budget, advising you on your wine list if you happen to have a restaurant and even match a wine to a special dish of yours. Deliveries take place in the major metropolitan area of Cape Town. Neil and Sue Proudfoot operate Wine Concepts on Kloof Street.

Wine Concepts – Newlands
Cardiff Castle Building
Corner Main Street & Kildare Road
Newlands 7700
Tel: +27-21-671-9030
Fax: +27-21-671-9031

Web: www.wineconcepts.co.za
Email:newlandshop@wineconcepts.co.za

Wine Concepts – Gardens
Shop 15, Lifestyles on Kloof
50 Kloof Street
Gardens 8001
Tel: +27-21-426-4401
Fax: 088-021-426-4401
Web: www.wineconcepts.co.za
Email: kloofst@wineconcepts.co.za

Vaughan Johnson operates his eponymous Wine and Cigar Shop on the Waterfront the Pierhead at the V & A Waterfront. Again someone who really knows his wines and offers a great service. Vaughan does a lot of business with the passengers on the ocean liners visiting the city.

Vaughan Johnson's Wine and Cigar Shop
V & A Waterfront Pierhead
Cape Town 8001
Tel: +27-21-419-2121
Fax: +27-21-419-0040
Web: www.vaughanjohnson.com
Email vjohnson@mweb.co.za

Caroline Rillema's Fine Wine Shops in Strand Street and on the Waterfront have an excellent offering which includes imported wines and glassware. Her annual Red and White Wine Reviews are well worth attending.

Caroline's Fine Wine Cellar
44 Matador Centre
62 Strand Street
Cape Town 8001
Tel: +27-21-419-8984
Fax: +27-21-419-8985
Web: www.carolineswine.com
Email caroline@carolineswine.com

V & A Waterfront
Tel: +27-21-425-5701
Fax: +27-21-425-5702

Ultra Liquors
Main Road
Wynberg
Cape Town
marknorrish@ultraliquors.co.za

Grand World of Wines
Convention Square
1 Lower Long street
Cape Town
8001
South Africa
email: jabspice@iafrica.com

Aroma Alphen Cellars
Constantia Village
Constantia Main Road
Constantia, Cape Town
Michael Schoeman -
alphen@aroma.co.za
Tel: +27-21-794-3143

Preston's
Main Road
Walmer
Port Elizabeth
presmel@santa-lucia.co.za
Tel: +27-41-581-1993
Also in East London & Bloemfontein

Gauteng

Solly Kramer and Carrie Adams run a
really brilliant wine shop in Illovo and
a satellite in the Hyde Park Shopping
Centre. They are very knowledgeable,
energetic and busy people and
will deliver even to Pretoria. Great
selection of wines, and spirits – and
single malts, beers and the rest.
Complete party package!

Norman Goodfellows
  Fine Wines & Spirits
192 Oxford Road
Illovo
Johannesburg
Tel: +27-11-788-4814

Norman Goodfellows
  Fine Wines & Spirits
Lower Ground Floor
Hyde Park Shopping Centre
Hyde Park
Tel: +27-11-325-6462
jeff@normangoodfellows.co.za

Bootleggers
Fourways Crossing
William Nicol Highway
Fourways
Johannesburg
bootleggers@mweb.co.za
Tel: +27-21-465-9777

Solly Kramers
c/o 4th Avenue & 6th Street
Parkhurst 2193
Johannesburg.
trl@icon.co.za
Tel: +27-11-788-0102

Johnny's Hyperliquor
Atterbury Value Mart
Atterbury Road

Faerie Glen 0042
Pretoria
mandy@johnnysliquors.co.za
Tel: +27-12-991-4999

Durban

Lance and Myles Buxton operate their
specialist wine shop from La Lucia
and deliver to the main metropolitan
are of Durban.

La Cave
La Lucia Mall
La Lucia, Durban
Tel: +27-31-572-6073
Email: lbuxton@mweb.co.za

Guy Dudley
Faerie Glen Liquors
Marine Drive
Margate
South Coast
Natal
fairieglen@tiscali.co.za

The Wine Cellar
Margie Spowart
Old Main Rd (R103),
Rosetta,
Natal Midlands
Tel +27 33 267 7044,
info@thewinecellar.co.za

Kath Gant
The Wine Registry
084 784 2408
info@thewineregistry.co.za
www.thewineregistry.co.za

I RAISE A GLASS TO

- My loved daughter Amy who helped me with the research for this book. Thank you darling for all you did for me.
- My publishers Gwynne Conlyn and Helen Holyoake, thank you for the invitation to do this book and the hand holding.
- Petal Palmer and Matthew Ibbotson, for another exercise in the fun of designing a book together.
- Special thanks to Russel Wasserfall for some great times shooting the pics for this book and for his brilliant photography. And to Yvette Pascoe the food stylist who set the shots up for us.
- Maureen Barnes who got me into writing in the first place, who is my gentlest critic and mentor.
- My friends in the wine public relations business, Gudrun Clarke, Tessa de Kock, Marlene Truter, Janie van der Spuy, Ian and Lisa Manley, Ian and Errieda du Toit, Beryl Eichenberger, Posy and Jeremy Hazell, Jeremy Nel, Shirley de Kock, Janice and Michael Fridjhon, Marius Labuschagne, Mariann Shinn and anyone else whose name I may have left out.
- Sheila Cosgreave, my partner in wine at Pick 'n Pay, who has taught me so much – and not only about wine. And for the laughs we've had.
- To the legendary Frank Swainston of Constantia Uitsig and also to Brendan Crew and Jean-Yves Muller of Caveau in Newlands for allowing us to invade their premises for the photography sessions.

index